Alive for Now

Using **Death** as a Teacher to Thrive in **Life**

Class 3/10/19

translated video:

1st event of death: grandfather dying as child (Dad's dad)

5 other events: - guinea pig Betsey/ comforting my Dad

• How changed?
• what I learned?

- Gabriel (Irish Setter) put to sleep when I was in school

- Missy's grandchild's birth

- Brooklyn cat heart attack (Tyson)

JESSICA MURBY

- Green Burial
- Artfull Ashes
- At a Journal Workshop (bk) by Ira Progoff

- Dad's death 3 years ago

To Maui, for her beautiful and magical ways that never fail to reveal truth,
spirit, and all that needs to be seen.

CONTENTS

The Dalai Lama, when asked what surprised him most about humanity, answered "Man.... because he sacrifices his health in order to make money. Then he sacrifices money to recuperate his health. And then he is so anxious about the future that he does not enjoy the present; the result being that he does not live in the present or the future; he lives as if he is never going to die, and then dies having never really lived."

Acknowledgements

Thank you to Laura Miner, for being there when it mattered most, encouraging this work, and being such a lovely example of what it means to "dance with death" and live life. Laura Seddon, my life wouldn't be anything close to what it has become without you, you've taught me to level up my life, how to trust, and you're always the one to call on when life gets real. My brave and loving mother, Robin Murby, for making multiple sacrifices to be by my side through my illness and surgery, and for never failing to exemplify what love really means. Amanda and John Mcquaid, for having me at your place after seven years of my being away, spending time with you and your beautiful babies has been healing and life affirming. Angie Hofmann for being my partner in crime, my host, cooking teacher, and entrepreneur of aloha consult. All of the people I've lived with for putting up with my introverted cubby holes of writing, including Grant Thompson for hosting and affirming the importance of this work. My acro yoga community for balancing all the work with play; especially Chris Taylor for your work in collaborating and facilitating trust in myself and our community. Zoe Wells for the inspiring conversations that lead to ideas and action. Aunties Joanie and Suzanne for your fun-loving nature and support. Willow Lisowski for being a never-ending source of encouraging words. Joan and Tomas Heartfield for teaching me how to thrive in life and love through writing a new story. Lucian Davis for your phone calls. Brittany Gibbs for being a loyal friend no matter how far apart we are. Auntie Linda Miccio for your adventurous and loving spirit. John Murby for your willingness to bring family together despite the challenges. Greg LaGoy for diagnosing my rare and freakish tumor. Anna Murphy for sharing your gifts with others, our initial conversations seemed to jumpstart this wild journey. All of the brave "Alive for Now" pilot program participants. The friends and training at Hospice Maui which led to the creation of much of this work. The Maui No Ka Oi Toastmasters group for being incredibly helpful and supportive. Kalani Retreat Center and all of my friends there for introducing many ways to thrive in life that I'd never before experienced. The National Institutes of Health for the dedication and expert medical care that's allowing myself and so many others to live and breathe right now. And finally, to the many patients, strangers, fellow zebras, friends, and relatives that have shared their life experiences and vulnerabilities with me.

Preface

The need for this work in using death as a teacher came from a few unexpected places. I had never anticipated or even imagined that my life would lead me to developing anything on this subject. It's as if I was uncovering a mystery over the course of many years that I wasn't aware I was trying to solve.

The most powerful factor leading to this work was discovering that I have an extremely rare condition that causes freakish tumors that produce adrenaline. This condition, called Paraganglioma, went undiagnosed as I experienced symptoms that felt like I was being chased for over a year. I had a constant high heart rate, high blood pressure, high blood sugar, excessive sweating, visual problems, and a general feeling of dread. I went to eight different doctors over the course of many months with no diagnosis. I finally shared my symptoms with my boss, the CEO of Hospice Maui, who correctly diagnosed the condition in an instant. Having that conversation with him truly saved my life because these tumors can be fatal not only in the traditional way of becoming metastatic, but the heart rate and blood pressure elevations that occur can lead to stroke, heart attack, and sudden death. That risk also makes surgery particularly dangerous. I ended up fleeing the managed care group in Hawaii that was refusing to pay for a surgeon that specializes in this condition. Through a series of miraculous events, I was accepted into a program at the National Institutes of Health (N.I.H.) in Maryland. I had the tennis ball sized tumor -which I named demon baby- removed at N.I.H., and I'm now a participant in a lifelong research study there. Most people I mention this to want to know what this may mean for my future, but because these tumors are such a mystery, they can't be tested for malignancy like other cancers can. Certain genetic factors lead to a higher rate of recurrence and metastases, and I discovered that I also have the "bad gene," which means a higher probability of more tumors. I really don't know what my future will look like in regards to this illness. I share such details because, for one, I feel that I've been given a second chance at life. Had I not discovered the cause of my symptoms or had the option to have expert care, it's likely I wouldn't be here right now. This is a gift in that I now deeply consider the preciousness of life and how I spend each moment. At the same time, I now live with knowing that this could recur and spread, that this condition could be what I die from. This has been a serious emotional challenge to navigate, yet it also informs the way I live in many unexpected and even positive ways. The perspective that I've gained through this experience has inspired much of this work.

Another major factor that led to this writing is only clear now in retrospect. Prior to this demonous tumor showing up and my working for hospice, I was fascinated and perplexed for years by what I can only describe as a rarity for humans to truly thrive in life, myself included. I wondered things like: "Why is it so rare that I find anyone that seems to be in a relationship or job that is healthy and fulfilling?" "Why aren't we having more fun?" "Why is it often so difficult for us to be nice to one another?" The potential implications of those unanswered questions became apparent to me from my meeting many people closer to the end of their lives in my work as an Occupational Therapist. For example, while working in the hospital, I met countless people that were finally reaching their retirement, just to sustain a debilitating illness or injury moments prior to "living the life they always wanted." Oftentimes, they'd comment on how living the life they *didn't* want is what led to the poor quality of life they had by the time I met them. The hard truth was that I saw my life going down that same path had I continued on the trajectory I was on. In addition, *all* the elders I met, even those who seemed to be fulfilled, shared that life was passing them by fast, far faster than they ever anticipated it would. It quickly became apparent to me that waiting to live life in any way could have serious consequences, yet it was still incredibly difficult to do what was necessary to make change. I didn't initially presume that this phenomenon had anything to do with a relationship to death, but I now suspect that it has everything to do with it. ***We don't have forever to start living the lives we are capable of, but it seems to be easy to act like we do***. The conclusion I've come to all these years later through navigating illness and working for hospice is: ***if we're not in touch with death, if we treat it as taboo, then of course it'd be easy to act as if we have forever, and to wait for a time that never actually comes to start living.***

The final and most intense reason that I'll state for creating this is because of how being in touch with death throughout life may inform the way we die. Through my experiences of working both in the hospital and hospice, I've found that there are too many questions that can go unanswered when these matters are kept in the shadow, which can lead to rifts in relationships, futile treatment efforts, trauma, and unnecessary suffering. That is in addition to the inherent difficulties that are already bound to arise for a dying person and their loved ones. Exploring death has the potential to bring great gifts which can improve both the way we live and die, gifts that otherwise can quite easily go a lifetime unrealized.

Implementing the awareness of death into our lives may be the most valuable tool we have for living fully. It is the most accelerated way to get in touch with our truest priorities and, most importantly, get our actions in line with them. This is a workbook to do just that. The journey you are about to take part in has the potential to be truly life changing.

How it Works

This workbook includes personal, weekly practices to be completed over a course of three months. The time frame is a metaphor for giving yourself *three months to live*, yet being very much alive, perhaps more alive than ever, by the end of that time. These practices involve contemplating and taking action to enrich life through addressing various things that can easily be avoided for a lifetime. Completing this work on a weekly basis, perhaps the same day each week, can help to integrate the material into your life. Mark your end date here and on your calendar three months from today in order to dedicate yourself to the weekly practices for this time period.

Today's date:_____

End date:_____

Week One

Seeing the End of all Things

Endings are true in love, in fear of change, in birth, in choosing to create anything, in all of the unknown that is with us constantly. I had an epiphany one day, which I now refer to as "seeing the end of all things." Shortly after I had my tumor removed in 2016, I got the call that there was a possibility that it could return and spread due to genetics. I felt sick over this news for days, I didn't know how I'd go on living while knowing that this could happen. Then, for the first time in my life, I finally allowed my mind to go to the **end** of what I was feeling when it came to something so frightening. As I allowed this to go on in my mind, at first I had horrible thoughts, but after a short time, my mind shifted into curiosity. I wondered, "How does it make any sense to feel like I can't go on living because I'm afraid I'm going to die? And, since dying is inevitable, how do I feel about death?" While contemplating this, I was amazed by the feeling of liberation that came over me. Knowing this information about the tumor has ultimately changed my life for the better. It informs the way I live everyday, which now leads me to consider what it may mean for us all to really let ourselves go to that place of "seeing the end of all things."

Life is interesting in that our survival and ability to thrive depend partly on our connections to one another; yet, death comes with the deal of being alive, which ultimately means saying goodbye to one another. Impermanence in the form of change and endings is also persistent throughout life, as much as it may be tempting to divert that truth. When we do attempt to resist change and try to make certain that which can't be so, our attempts can be destructive; we can try to secure a person by using tactics to keep them around, we can manipulate a situation to keep it static, we can ignore a greater calling due to not wanting to get out of our comfort zone, we can torture ourselves by trying to hold onto the past. All of which can actually lead to further disconnection and stagnation.

How do we both live and love when nothing will last? I believe in order to really love anything means to simultaneously surrender it, let go of it, to see its end. And to thrive in life means to see its end as well. ***Our love of everything includes its inevitable end in one way or another. Instead of that making it all meaningless, maybe it's the very thing that makes life and love worth it.***

The power of endings can show up strongly when impending change is obvious. Many people refer to a phenomenon that occurs when they're just about to leave a place or situation, a capacity to be more courageous, more authentic than usual. That they're more apt to try something new, to act in a way that doesn't match their image, to pursue someone or something they're interested in. I think that what we're capable of in those moments hints at what truly living is, and that the capacity to live in that way is always inherent within us since death is inevitable, that is as long as we're willing to remember that truth.

<u>**Week One Practice**</u>

1) Can you "see the end" of everything and everyone you engage with this week, as you do so? This includes everything you own, the people in your life, your work, etc. Can you attempt to surrender all that you love and be with it at the same time? Note if anything changes as a result.

2) Is there something in life that you've been particularly afraid of and resistant to let yourself think about? Can you "see it through to the end" in your mind? If so, record your process here.

Week Two

"Do anything, but let it produce joy."
~Walt Whitman

What Makes you Feel Alive?

"Go after your passion as if your life depends on it…"

…Those were the words of an 82-year-old woman that was a patient of mine. She died shortly after we met.

Her words likely felt so potent and have stayed with me because it was so clear that she had truly lived by them. I'd never before met someone who seemed to be so comfortable with their own death, especially when it was coming so close. It was undeniable from my perspective that she had thrived in her life, particularly when it came to pursuing what she was passionate about. She wrote books, taught at universities, traveled the world, and only married once she found true love. That is not to presume that the ways of living she chose are ideal for all people, but that there was no doubt that she had lived intentionally by engaging in what made ***her*** feel truly alive.

So the question is…

Do you engage in those things that make *you* feel truly alive?

Engaging in what one is passionate about seems to be a common means to accessing that feeling of being truly alive. Passion, to me, is defined as anything that lights you up inside, and that on some level you may feel "called to." Do you feel called to create something? Volunteer for a cause? Start a business? Share something? The things that we are passionate about also tend to ironically be those that bring up the most resistance, fear, and inhibition within us to initiate. Furthermore, they tend to be easily dismissed in society if they are not traditional, and viewed as impractical, luxurious pursuits. Yet, I find engaging in them to be the very means to allow us to serve others in the most meaningful and impactful way. I find that not doing so is a bigger sacrifice, to sacrifice one's true self and to deprive others that could benefit from that work. Our desires towards certain things arise for a reason, and it's a bigger deal than it's often made out to be to ignore them. ***It is not a luxury, but a responsibility we have to engage in our passions, in order for us to contribute to the greater good of the world, in whatever unique way that may be.***

Maintaining an awareness of death is the best catalyst I know to initiate pursuing our passions despite the challenges. It may sound extreme to remind ourselves of death in order to take action on something that really matters to us in life. However, when acknowledging death's inevitable truth, it in a way makes perfect sense that a reminder of it is the "extreme" we need to act despite the level of resistance that can be present.

<u>Week Two Practice</u>

1) Would you like to make more time for that which makes you feel alive?

2) Have you had a recurring feeling about pursuing something in life in particular?

3) If you're not sure if you'd like to initiate something, the "deathbed check" can help you to get clear on what matters. Imagining yourself on your deathbed, does it feel important to pursue this or not?

4) Take time to explore and work on something you are passionate about for 15-30 minutes each day this week if this is applicable to you.

Week Three

"Death is not waiting for us at the end of a long road. Death is always with us, in the marrow of every passing moment. She is the secret teacher hiding in plain sight, helping us to discover what matters most."
~Frank Ostaseski

Unwinding

It feels most relevant to include addressing the relationships in our lives in this journey, as these connections are often revealed to be paramount when a person is dying. Eugene O'Kelly spent the last few months of his life writing a book titled "Chasing Daylight: How My Forthcoming Death Transformed My Life." He started writing this book after being diagnosed with brain cancer, and being given a life expectancy of three months. Not only did he complete the book in that time frame, he also completed a process in which he addressed and resolved each relationship in his life. He called this process "Unwinding."

"...the exercise forced me to do the very thing that wiser people every now and then advise us to do- that is, to stop and look up long enough to think about the people we love and why we love them, and to go and tell them *explicitly* how we feel, because who knows when that opportunity will disappear forever?"

"It made me think that other people, especially those with much more than three months left (for example, several decades), could benefit from the approach I took, or at least modify it to make it their own."

As he completed this process of resolving relationships, *__he wondered why he had waited so long, and why it took the extreme of late stage brain cancer to do this.__* I believe we can all benefit from this process (which is outlined in detail in the next practice) now. Ironically, it can take courage to address even the positive feelings we have for others. It is also common to assume people know how we feel, when they don't actually know the depths of it unless it is communicated.

<u>Week Three Practice</u>

1) Choose three people, perhaps from different "circles" of your life.

2) Reflect on each person and recall, in the closest detail possible, the moments the two of you have enjoyed together.

3) Choose which means feels best to communicate with each person: a meeting, phone call, video call, email, letter, etc.

4) Share with them:

    • The qualities in them you particularly appreciate:

    • The lessons you've learned by knowing them:

•The ways in which they've inspired you most:

•The greatest memories you've had with them:

•Anything else that feels pertinent:

Note: It may be helpful to use the "deathbed check" as a barometer for this practice. Since we never really know, consider what you would wish were said if you did not have another moment as you respond to the above prompts.

If you want a way to approach others with this, you can preface it with this:

"I'm completing an exercise from a workbook called 'Alive for Now' in which I 'check in' with a few important people in my life. This is in the spirit of not taking things for granted, or assuming we'll have forever to communicate these things. I'd like to use this as an opportunity that many don't take until very late in their lives, if ever. This was inspired by a man that completed this process with each of his friends and family members as he was dying, and then wished he had done so long before he was sick. I also want you to know that I'm okay, I have no apparent pressing need to tell you these things, but I'm choosing to take this opportunity to let you know."

Week Four

"...when we finally know we are dying, and all other sentient beings are dying with us, we start to have a burning, almost heartbreaking sense of the fragility and preciousness of each moment and each being, and from this can grow a deep, clear, limitless compassion for all beings."
~Sogyal Rinpoche

Gratitude

I invite you to place the following aspects of life in order of their importance to you…

Your ability to:

Walk

Get Dressed

Go to the bathroom

Shower

Remember

Communicate

Eat

Your three most important roles:

1) _____

2) _____

3) _____

The three closest people to you:

1) _____

2) _____

3) _____

Your three favorite activities:

1) _____

2) _____

3) _____

It is likely very difficult to place those in order of importance. I ask you to do so anyway because the proportion of appreciation we often feel for those things is not at all equal to the amount of loss we'd feel if they were gone. Which indicates a bit of a predicament: **as human beings, it's as if we have a default state of forgetting all the incredible things we are granted with as we live our lives.** This can ironically and most often hold true for those individuals who are granted the most comforts, such as many of us living in the western world. We seem to have a particular opposition to losing these things with time, as if we are owed them, as if losing them is unnatural. Yet, the truth is that all of us are vulnerable to losing them at any time. In the training I completed at Hospice Maui, we were guided through a powerful practice which reminded us that the people we visit are in the process of being deprived of each of their abilities, relationships, and roles, regardless of what they'd choose to let go of first. That practice, as well as a daily gratitude practice, has personally helped me immensely in maintaining the greater perspective of all of the abilities and comforts I have access to.

We all have moments in which we tap into all the miracles that are occurring to allow us to function, and in those moments we can feel immense appreciation. One vehicle for that may be when we experience a "close call," or when something is lost, even if it's only temporary, like when we're injured or have a cold. I feel it's best we find a way to be more aware of our blessings now, before we're grieving the loss of them. It always seems to hurt that much more when we feel the absence of something we never quite pondered the transience of or appreciated enough. Cultivating a gratitude practice can allow us to become *hyperaware* of all the things in life that are so easily taken for granted.

Week Four Practice

1) Write down five things that you are grateful for every night before you go to bed this week. Make it non-negotiable: even if you don't feel like it, and especially if you don't feel grateful in that moment, find just five things you are genuinely grateful for, no matter how small. It may be something easily overlooked, such as an interesting conversation. If you feel like writing more than five once you start, then keep going. You can start here:

         1. _____

         2. _____

         3. _____

         4. _____

         5. _____

2) Note your independence as you use the functions you have: as you eat, communicate with people, stand up, get dressed, shower, etc.

3) Consider all that allowed you to simply survive each of your days: the access you have to the things that keep you alive such as food and water, that you made it through your commute unharmed, all of the comforts that you've become used to: a home, warm showers, and a bed to sleep in.

Week Five

"Every moment of light
and dark is a miracle."
~Walt Whitman

Exploring Regret

A Hospice Nurse named Bronnie Ware shared what she discovered to be common regrets of dying people in her popular blog turned book titled "The Top Five Regrets of the Dying." What I think is important to note with her work is that identifying these regrets was not something she had originally set out to do, she had simply heard these so frequently and repeatedly from the dying people she cared for that she felt compelled to share them. The regrets she identified are often surprising to people:

1) **I wish I'd had the courage to live a life true to myself, not the life others expected of me.**
2) **I wish I hadn't worked so hard.**
3) **I wish I'd had the courage to express my feelings.**
4) **I wish I had stayed in touch with my friends.**
5) **I wish that I had let myself be happier.**

It can be an incredibly powerful practice to reflect on each of these regrets. Many aspects of these ways of living -happy, true to oneself, vulnerable- are not actually easy. As ironic as it is, it can take a great amount of courage to simply be authentic. It can be a helpful practice to check in and consider what you may regret if your time was short. Looking at your life exactly as it is now, which of those may be on your regret list if you didn't have much time left?

Part of me doesn't actually believe in regret, because growth and wisdom may not be possible without reflecting on those things we would choose to do differently with time. It seems to be in life's nature to look back at things we did last year or last week or a minute ago with the potential to be perplexed by our own actions. The great challenge for many of us is to reconcile the fact that it is not possible to go back in time to change what's been done; to say something different, to prevent the accident, to eat better, to prevent the cancer, to avoid that relationship. Reconciling that can be particularly difficult in regards to serious tragedies. Part of the beauty and richness of life is what can come next; the willingness to have the difficult conversations, to say sorry, to recognize our imperfect behavior, to forgive others and ourselves, to surrender to what happens in life even if we can't make sense of it. In my opinion, it behooves us to attempt to do so before our time left is short.

Contemplating the reality of these regrets -and the reality death in general- can be a catalyst to take action on what we know is important; to stop using excuses, to let go of long-held grudges, to have the courage to pursue our true passions in life, to share the truest parts of ourselves that we're afraid we may be rejected for, and so on, despite having fear.

<u>Week Five Practice</u>

1) If any of those regrets have the potential to be true for you, what is one thing you can do this week to address them? Perhaps to…

- Initiate a potentially difficult conversation?

- Reach out to someone you've been out of touch with?

- Pursue a passion that has been calling you?

- Show interest in someone?

- Speak your truth?

Note: Using the practice of imagining yourself on your deathbed may help you to gather some strength to do something you feel resistance to do in the moment. If you feel fear, I encourage you to ask yourself, what would you regret more, even with the risk of an unfavorable outcome, taking action or not taking action?

2) Is it time for you to reconcile something from the past that you regret? It may not be possible to take any action to fix what has happened, but simply take this time to consider that this is something that we all need to work with. This may be a good week to open up to a person you trust, or to get the help you need "let go," and to forgive yourself or others.

Week Six

"The dark does not destroy the light; it defines it. It's our fear of the dark that casts our joy into the shadows."
~Brené Brown

The Dark Side of Positivity

Valuing the positive aspects of life seems to be the standard today; a focus on happiness, optimism, positive thinking, as well as the general social norm of keeping conversations to uplifting topics. It's almost considered bad manners to answer the question of "how are you?" with any mention of struggle, sadness, or grief.

I've experienced the benefits of optimism and intention very much in my own life, which is why I was shocked when I began to notice a theme of this approach to life being a culprit of much distress for those experiencing circumstances that are considered "dark," such as having an illness, dying, or simply going through anything that is considered undesirable.

Some examples of the dark side of positivity:

- A person experiencing a serious illness or other problem feels dejected or even alienated by others due to being told by numerous people that they are manifesting their issue, and to switch to more positive thoughts.

- A person feels guilt, insecurity, or lack of confidence for being diagnosed with a terminal illness, other ailment, or even for dying. They may not be able to identify exactly why they're experiencing these emotions, but feel as though they have done something "wrong."

- Someone experiencing grief is demanded to "show up" in a culture that expects happiness, emotional control, and productivity, adding to their suffering and complicating their process.

- When the truth of having a terminal illness is avoided by individuals and loved ones, resulting in a failure to appreciate the moments that are left.

- When speaking out loud about death is considered dangerous, as if it's bad luck or unnatural, leading to lack of preparedness throughout life.

- ***When we say we're "good" when we're really something more like depressed, anxious, on the brink of divorce, etc., which leads to us feeling more depressed, which in turn makes others who are feeling all of those things feel worse too because they think our lives are so great.***

Since sadness, struggle, endings, and death are a natural part of life, how is it that we've made them out to be deficiencies? Many would deny that we've made them out to be deficiencies, which is why I've compiled the examples above. I don't believe it's always a conscious issue. It's more often kept in the shadow, a faith in positivity being one reason it remains there.

This issue seems to become apparent to a person once they've experienced something cataclysmic, as I have heard such common examples from many individuals in the midst of illness, dying, and grief.

The positive approach certainly appears to be valuable and supportive, which may be the reason it can be so insidious. As profound the effects of a positive mentality can be, the problem I find with it is that it's only *half* of the truth of the reality of life, and not applicable to everything. Darkness is just as present as light here on earth, even literally- like how there is a sunset for every sunrise, joy *and* pain wavering in every one of us, death being part of the deal with every birth, impermanence presenting itself constantly.

It may be best for us to explore this reality of the full spectrum of life now; including what is dark or undesirable, considering that significant challenges will arise for each and every one of us. And with that, it may be serving for us to give ourselves and one another space to explore the feelings that arise when we do.

Death and grief and illness may not even be inherently negative, perhaps they may have a meaning beyond what we can comprehend as we're in the midst of them. Maybe if we got everything we wanted in the way of positivity we wouldn't have any growth. ***By making these parts of life out to be failures, we may fail to truly live and be there for one another.***

Week Six Practice

1) Can you identify any instances in which you have experienced the "dark side of positivity?"

2) Do you find yourself naturally more open or resistant to discuss others' unpleasant experiences?

3) Is there a "dark" emotion or circumstance that you've felt resistance within yourself to explore? Do you think there may be a benefit in allowing yourself to go there?

4) Have you ultimately realized any gifts from circumstances in the past that were dark or unpleasant as you were going through them?

Week Seven

"Your problem is, you
think you have time."
~Buddha

Forgiveness

Forgiveness can be a tricky topic. Relationships, especially amongst family members, can be extremely complicated. In Hospice, I've heard countless instances of family members spending decades not speaking to one another due to past turmoil, which is then addressed with urgency when a person has moments left to live. Sometimes people ultimately miss the chance to meet in person due to their loved one dying before their meeting. As much as I struggle with the subject of forgiveness myself, what has kept my efforts going is taking note of how ***people seem to change their minds and want to initiate contact at the end of one's life; what was an option the whole time suddenly becomes urgent.***

The fact that people spend decades out of contact in the first place also illustrates how terribly difficult it can be to reconcile and forgive. Which is why I feel it's paramount to address this here. It's another subject that can be easily avoided for a lifetime.

There's a lot of advice out there regarding forgiveness, yet it can be confusing. Some wonder why they should forgive when they were the ones "done wrong." Many people were children or in other vulnerable situations when damage occurred that continues to affect them later in life. We're often told to forgive despite the damage in order to live to our full potential. I agree with that, but the bigger question seems to be **_how_**. As much as the desire for peace seems to be present for so many of us, there may still be feelings of resentment.

Here is some of what I've taken away along my journey with forgiveness that I wish I had known sooner:

1) Forgiveness doesn't mean you have to engage in any unhealthy dynamics. You may feel it's not yet healthy to spend time with a person. Setting boundaries is especially important in regards to an abusive relative or past relationship.

2) Making peace with what you think should have been different in the past is a primary component in regards to moving forward, which may require consistent self-reminders.

3) Listening to more extreme stories of people forgiving others for what appears to be unforgivable can be an incredibly inspiring catalyst to take steps to forgive. Rwandan Holocaust survivor Immaculée Ilibagiza is one great example.

4) It's key to not avoid addressing these difficult relationships only because it's uncomfortable, because it's bound to be, this seems to be a large factor in the confrontation being avoided for so long.

5) Focusing on the ways in which the dynamic has positively contributed to who you have become can be helpful, as even the most undesirable

challenges seem to have the potential to do. The default seems to be to focus only on the hurt and negative effects that the dynamic has caused.

6) Seeking out a therapist or other professional for help can also be serving. In my experience, this can simply provide a more objective perspective.

7) When initiating these conversations, organizing thoughts ahead of time and waiting for a moment to confront things when not triggered seems to be ideal. Although in my experience, it doesn't always happen this way.

Week Seven Practice

If you'd like to address a complicated relationship or other forgiveness matter in your life this week, use your discretion as to who to do this with. As with the "Unwinding" practice, check in with what you think would be most important if either of you weren't here tomorrow. Use whatever means (writing, meeting, phone call, etc.) you feel is best.

Personal reflection questions:

1) What are the primary words that run through your mind when you think about this person or situation? What feelings arise when you do this?

2) Even if you can identify many ways in which this dynamic has negatively affected you, do you see any way in which even the most undesirable dynamic has <u>positively</u> contributed to who you are, be it courageous, empathetic, driven, etc.?

Prompts for communicating with another person:

1) Are there any "elephants in the room?" This is regarding what has not been communicated. What, if either of you had little time left, would be unsaid or unaddressed? What is it that you want to discuss in order to move forward?

2) What are the greatest memories you've had with this person? This question may be important to answer because when relationships are more difficult, it can be easy to go a long time without remembering the positive aspects of them as well. People can be shocked to hear the good memories if they are dealing with guilt about what "should" have been, or if they are used to only hearing about what they've done wrong.

3) It may be serving to let the person know the ways in which this relationship has been difficult for you, if applicable. I've personally been amazed by the benefits of stating this to others compassionately, especially when I assumed that they already had this understanding.

4) What you forgive them for:

5) What you'd like to ask forgiveness for:

6) What you'd like the relationship to look like moving forward:

7) Anything else that you'd like to express:

Note:

- You may choose to express all of this privately and not send it.

- If the person you're addressing has died, you can still do this exercise in whichever way you feel is best. Some people write letters, read them out loud to someone else, or visit a place that was meaningful to the person involved.

- There is some risk involved with this exercise, as it involves "rocking the boat." Some people may not respond or may respond negatively. Some may not like the directness of this exercise; it may not be your style either. You can adapt it to what feels best. Even if someone is dying, they are not always responded to with compassion. It's up to you if it's worth the risk of a changed relationship or a negative response. I say do what feels right while ensuring that you're safe and being respectful.

If you'd like a way to approach others with this, you can preface it with this:

"I'm completing a program called 'Alive for Now' and the exercise this week is on forgiveness. This is a time in which I address the relationships in my life that need attention. The purpose of this is to talk about those things that haven't been discussed but feel important to address, with the intention of settling things. It seems all too common for people to assume they have forever to communicate what's important. I'd like to use this as an opportunity that many don't take until very late in their lives, if ever. If you are interested in discussing these things with me further, please let me know."

Week Eight

"Life is continuously changing, and if you're trying to control it, you'll never be able to fully live it."
~Michael Singer

Death & Femininity

Education regarding how to care for dying people seems to always come down to one simple teaching: the ability to just ***be*** with people. Which brings about the question… why would that require training? And more importantly, why do we so easily discount the power of that?

We tend to place an immense amount of importance on having an answer, on doing something to fix a problem, on being in control, and making sense of everything. These are mainly masculine qualities. They are important qualities, and certainly have their place. A balance of those with feminine virtues is what I find to be dangerously lacking, which has been exemplified in a variety ways poignantly throughout history and uniquely now. ***The feminine is about embracing the mysteries, the paradoxes, about listening and surrendering, with so much that we discount yet that death asks of us, both in terms of being there for others and when our time comes.***

The often forgotten feminine virtues of
Paradox, Mystery, Listening, and Surrender:

Paradox

It can be difficult to hold two seemingly contradictory ideas to be true at the same time, yet paradoxes are everywhere. **Death** can be horrible and yet can be beautiful in a way that's often likened to birth. **Grief** can feel absolutely unbearable and can impede with even the most basic life tasks, yet has the capacity to change a person for the better. Being a **caregiver** can be a burden and an honor all at the same time.

A friend of mine once confided in me that right after her mom died, she ran into her dad's bedroom and excitedly exclaimed, "she did it!" and immediately felt that her relief for her mother -which prompted that- was perhaps inappropriate. She shared that it seemed to have made her dad feel uncomfortable, which then caused her to feel wrong for it. This is just one example of a person suppressing the full spectrum of how they truly feel around dying, as if having the positive feelings of relief or excitement means they can't simultaneously be grieving and holding the "negative" feelings of longing and sadness for their loved one.

I find it to be a gift to embrace these paradoxes, that doing so allows freedom for one to explore their true feelings without being wrong or irrational for it. The masculinity of logic says we choose one and not the other. The intuitive feminine side says we can hold them both simultaneously.

Mystery

Death is often referred to as a great mystery. The necessity to come to a conclusion about all things removes the possibility of embracing mystery. This may be a culprit of the potentially hurtful responses individuals make to try to make sense of another person's illness or death, such as blaming the cause on their fear, or being too passive, or the person needing to be somewhere else. I'm not implying that those aren't possibilities, but that the very nature of these quick answers hint at our discomfort in embracing the feminine aspect of being with and accepting the unknowable. These answers, although likely well-intended, can hinder a grieving or ill or dying person from overtly exploring these mysteries for themselves. By embracing mysteries, we can simply openly share ideas without the need to come to a conclusion, which in turn invites others to openly question and marvel in the unknown.

<u>Listening</u>

I'd often heard while working in healthcare how much simply listening to others is helpful, and while I would often take time to do so, I never really gave it much credit. Being sick myself has allowed me to understand the level at which that is true. I didn't realize the magic of this until I was on the receiving end when I really needed it. Being with a person who is actually being present and willing to listen without trying to fix anything can be a great gift. As uncomfortable as we may be with it, and as little credit we may give it, ***being in that unknown, uncomfortable place with a person can do wonders for them beyond what we may imagine.***

<u>Surrender</u>

Surrendering to what is happening can be a difficult task, especially in those places and cultures in which the majority consider a lack of control to be a weakness. Dying and the loss of one's abilities at some point give a person no choice but to surrender.

I believe it serves us to at least start to reflect on this now, before the time comes that we get the terminal diagnosis, before we are needing to depend on others due to the inevitabilities of aging and dying ourselves.

We may better prepare for this time now by finding a balance of being and doing, listening and expressing, giving and receiving, and of surrender and control. And by doing so, I'll bet that we live better in the process.

Exploring this balance is not only for the benefit of oneself, but also for when the time comes for us to be with someone else as they are dying. To trust that holding that space is courageous and powerful and important and healing. Especially when we get to that inevitable place in which there is nothing we can ***do.***

<u>Week Eight Practice</u>

This week, simply explore that balance within yourself. Do you tend to feel more comfortable with:

- **being vs. doing?**
- **giving vs. receiving?**
- **listening vs. expressing?**
- **surrendering vs. controlling?**

There's no need to "do" any specific task, just take note of these polarities and consider how they display themselves in your everyday life, and in turn how that may affect you and your loved ones in regards to living and dying.

Week Nine

*"Do everything as if it were the last
thing you were doing in your life."*
~Marcus Aurelius

Advance Directives

~This information is not a substitute for legal advice~

The most practical form of making plans in regards to quality of life is likely to complete an Advance Directive, which is a legal document in which you have the opportunity to specify which actions should be taken for your health if you are no longer able to make decisions for yourself, and who you would like to assign to make those decisions.

An Advance Directive doesn't usually require much information, yet allows an individual to answer some incredibly important questions regarding what is important to them in critical moments.

The **Five Wishes** is one form of an Advance Directive. I prefer this one because it includes important questions beyond the basics and I like the aesthetic of it. Some people prefer their state's directive, which is often available to print online at no cost. The Five Wishes meets the legal requirements for an Advance Directive in 42 U.S. states including Hawaii. In the other eight states, the completed Five Wishes can be attached to the state's required form.

The Five Wishes include:

1) The Person I Want to Make Care Decisions for Me When I Can't

2) The Kind of Medical Treatment I Want or Don't Want

3) How Comfortable I Want to Be

4) How I Want People to Treat Me

5) What I Want My Loved Ones to Know

Why Advance Directives are Important (regardless of your age or health status):

- Fundamentally, completing an Advance Directive can save you from potential suffering in regards to receiving the kind of treatment that you **do** want, and not having treatment that you **don't** want.

- Regardless of if or how it ever needs to be used, it can be a conversation starter between you and your family, friends, doctor, etc. It can spark some very riveting discussions about life and provide instant insight and perspective as to what matters.

- Family members and others in your life can potentially have the peace of mind in honoring your desires as opposed to the potential trauma and rifts that can happen between them when having to guess what you want.

- If your family and friends complete theirs, it can give you peace of mind as well.

I hadn't completed my own Advance Directive -even with realizing their importance through working in both the hospital and hospice settings- until I was diagnosed with a life-threatening illness and knew I was going to need to have surgery. When I was meeting with the intake coordinator at the hospital I was admitted to, she began to educate me about Advance Directives without asking if I had one, she noted her surprise when I handed mine over. It felt so good to have completed it prior to that visit, especially in that it eased some of my stress in preparation for surgery.

Advance Directives are appropriate for adults of all ages, the history of highly publicized life-support controversy cases that I am familiar with have actually been most often with younger adults.

<u>**Week Nine Practice**</u>

1) Don't wait! If you choose, **fill out an Advance Directive** that you prefer (if you've already completed one, take this week to review and update it, if needed). If you are interested in The Five Wishes, it is easy to obtain online at a small cost.

2) If you like, **attach a personal page** in your own words clarifying how you define quality of life, what you'd like others to know in the case they need to use the form, or anything else you feel is pertinent to add.

3) Be sure to **follow instructions** on who to share this with and where to keep it.

4) **Share your experience**. You may be surprised to learn how many people you know haven't completed or updated theirs, and you can be a catalyst for them to do so. Some people even choose to get together with others to get this done.

Note: When it comes to the paramedics following a person's wishes in an emergency situation, an Advance Directive is not pertinent. An Advance Directive can be of use though after that emergency treatment has been given in regards to what to do next. A different form, which contains orders for life sustaining treatment (called a POLST in Hawaii, the name of this varies state to state) is required in emergency situations, and is only an option for individuals who are seriously ill.

Week Ten

"We were together.
I forget the rest."
~Walt Whitman

Honoring Loved Ones

One of the things I loved most from the hospice training I completed was recognizing that we can take time to honor loved ones that have died before us **anytime** we'd like. Each of us in the training simply shared some words to memorialize a person in our lives that has died, which was actually very powerful. I didn't realize something like this would be serving for me (beyond a funeral or other service) until I was given the unique opportunity to do so formally in a group. It felt natural, and was even enjoyable, not just in my own process, but in witnessing what transpired in others as they did the same.

This likely felt so therapeutic because of the undeniable connection we have to our loved ones even after they're gone; our parents, grandparents, ancestors being a literal part of who we are. It seems that in modern society we've become generally more disconnected from our ancestors and roots. There also appears to be an increasingly hasty expectation for us to "move on" after a death, and to return to our previous lives in a culture that doesn't always hold space for mourning. Creating our ***own*** space to honor loved ones that have passed may be more important than ever.

Commemorating those that have died before us can be a great opportunity to:

- Process grief.

- Create a space to share what we might not have the opportunity to share in everyday conversation.

- Reclaim our natural ability and inklings to do so.

- Remain connected to our ancestry and lineage.

- Hold in gratitude the people that are presently alive around us.

- Again, be reminded of the inevitability of death.

<u>Week Ten Practice</u>

Be sure to have the time and support for processing emotions before initiating this practice, as it may bring up grief. As always, do what feels right for you and only in the right time.

1) Reflect on the loved ones that have died before you, and choose one person to honor this week.

2) If it feels pertinent, obtain an item that symbolizes the person to hold.

3) Sit in a place that in some way makes you feel connected to them; this may be a quiet space, or even a physical location that was significant to them.

4) Contemplate what this person has meant and means to you. In regards to relatives of earlier generations, it can be powerful to consider the sacrifices that they made that allow you to have the freedoms and life that you have.

5) Spend 5-10 minutes to convey either in words, in writing, or in your mind anything you feel like expressing in regards to this person.

6) If you'd like to do this process with a group of people, the same steps can be applied. Unlike more conventional ceremonies, it's not even necessary that you all gather to memorialize the *same* person, but to hold a space for each person to share some words regarding a person they each knew and loved. It can actually be quite powerful to be heard and witnessed, and to hear and witness others as they do the same.

Week Eleven

"Your legacy is every
life you've touched."
~Maya Angelou

What you Leave Behind

This week's practice is about making plans for **after** your death regarding your service and remains, and also what you personally want your loved ones to know after you die. This can allow others to have the peace of mind of being able to honor what you want, and can even save them time and energy by only utilizing the means that resonate with you. The questions below are also natural prompts to reflect on life up until this moment, and on the reality of death.

~Answering the questions below is not a substitute for completing a legal document, if you need legal advice, please consult a lawyer~

Your Name: _____

Today's date: _____

After my death, I want...

1) My remains

    a. Burial

    b. Cremation

    c. Green burial

    d. Ocean body burial

    e. Other: _____

How important this is to me (circle 0-5): 0   1   2   3   4   5

              (not important)   (very important)

2) Location(s) of my remains

_____

How important this is to me (circle 0-5): 0   1   2   3   4   5

              (not important)   (very important)

3) My service

    a. Funeral home

    b. Wake

    c. Faith-based ceremony: _____

    d. At-home funeral

    e. Celebration of life

    f. Intimate gathering

    g. Other: _____

How important this is to me (circle 0-5): 0   1   2   3   4   5

              (not important)   (very important)

Anything else for my loved ones to know regarding my desires for my remains and services after death:

What I want others to know most regarding *how I feel about life and death*:

My Eulogy (This may include your greatest qualities, how you've served, the hardest things about life and the greatest blessings. This doesn't need to be what is actually shared at your service; but for self-reflection, and possibly a guide others can use when writing your eulogy):

The first three things that come to my mind regarding what I've loved most about being alive (as of today):

1)

2)

3)

Anything else I want to be sure my loved ones know after I die:

Week Eleven Practice

1) Share your responses with the people in your life this week that may be involved with this planning. This can be in the form of writing or in conversation. Be sure to let them know that you have no pressing need to tell them at this moment, and that you're choosing to do so before the need to do so is urgent or undone. This may prompt them to share their plans as well.

2) This may also be a good week to create or update a document specifying the distribution of your belongings after you die, such as a will and trust, as these matters have the potential to cause major conflict between family members if not taken care of and discussed ahead of time.

Week Twelve

"Remembering that I'll be dead soon is the most important tool I've ever encountered to help me make the big choices in life. Almost everything -all external expectations, all pride, all fear of embarrassment or failure- these things just fall away in the face of death, leaving only what is truly important."

~Steve Jobs

Life Review

There's a sentiment that we've all likely heard from our elders: **life goes by fast, far faster than we can possibly anticipate as we're living it**. I've heard that from most everyone I've met while working in homecare, the hospital, and in hospice. The saying has even become a cliché, yet there's a deeper lesson in it that I can't ignore and feel is imperative we delve into now... **we don't have forever to start living the lives we truly want to live**... this may sound obvious, but I don't find it to be common for the majority of us to act as if it were true. If we did, then I believe we'd see more evidence of it; I believe it'd be more common for us to be kinder to one another, to be more present and full of wonder, to honor ourselves in the ways in which we spend the majority of our time; in our relationships, health, work, etc., despite our fears and our challenges. And what is the culprit of treating life as if it's endless? I believe it is in treating death as a taboo, that the more we keep it in the shadow, the less we recognize life's preciousness, and the less we can live our lives from a place of what truly matters.

Individuals who proclaim to have had near death experiences often report to not only make major changes in their lives afterwards, but also to realize in their life review that it was their seemingly *small* actions that had the greatest effect; a conversation, an act of generosity, a smile, etc. ***What matters most may be the innumerable opportunities we have to live to our true potential in every. single. moment.*** Yet, there are many aspects of life that can easily dominate our time and energy that reveal themselves to be unimportant when death comes close. The effects of this are not always clear until very late in one's life, as well as the realization of what a robbery of life that has been. Completing our own version of a life review now while considering the inevitability of death can be a great catalyst for us to take steps to live our lives from a place of what truly matters.

Week Twelve Practice

What have been the three of the greatest highlights of your life so far? Feel free to record the first three that come to your mind without thinking about this too much.

1)	2)	3)

Which of the categories of life included below do the highlights that you noted fall into?

Family	Social Life	Health
Service/Philanthropy	Work	Adventure/Travel
Love Life	Creativity/Passion	Other

The categories you chose above might hint at what you value most. ***Does the way that you currently spend your time truly reflect that which you value most?*** If you are ambitious, record how you actually spend your time for a typical 48 hours on a separate page to find out. Recording those details can be tedious but life altering.

What do you feel you owe to yourself to 'work on' while you're still here?

Write a mission statement for your life. There are no rules for doing this. Simply note what you are here to do and be:

What supports you in living by your mission (e.g. being surrounded the right people, exercising, etc.)?:

What hinders you from living by your mission (e.g. worrying about what other people think, neglecting mental and physical health, etc.)?:

List three specific & practical actions you can take this week to live by your life's mission:

1)	2)	3)

Lastly, I invite you to use this practice (and any other that you liked) as a means to give each moment you have left the attention and presence that it merits.

The End...

"What makes anything precious except that it ends?"
~Bj Miller

Congratulations! Completing this work is a courageous journey that can create positive and lasting transformation. Beyond these practices, death can continue to serve as a teacher anytime in life. It can be checked in with even in the small moments of taking action on anything that involves the subjects we covered here and beyond: to tell someone how you feel, to make important plans, to navigate regret, to forgive, to be present, to feel alive, to make it through dark times, etc.

The mystery I've felt compelled to share through my own illness and that of others' I've met along the way is that using death as a teacher can quite counterintuitively come with many great gifts, gifts that could otherwise go a lifetime unrealized. To be with anything while contemplating its death does not in turn make light of it, but somehow adds to its meaning, adds to life's purpose, increases our capacity to connect and feel and love in order to truly ***thrive in life***.

ABOUT THE AUTHOR

Jessica Murby is a Hospice Liaison, Occupational Therapist, lover of life, and acro yogi. She unexpectedly came upon the benefits of using death as teacher through her clinical experience and through navigating illness herself. She is part of a lifelong research study at the National Institutes of Health (N.I.H.). Jessica currently splits her time between her roots in New England and the beautiful island of Maui. She also shares her unique work through public speaking, retreats, and workshops.

Find out more at:
JessicaMurby.com
Facebook.com/AliveforNowBook
Instagram.com/jessimaui

Bibliography

Week Three: Unwinding

O'Kelly, E. O'Kelly, C. (2008) *Chasing Daylight: How My Forthcoming Death Transformed My Life.* New York, NY: McGraw-Hill.

Week Four: Gratitude

The practice at the beginning of this chapter was adapted from what I remember of a profound exercise that was led by <u>Greg LaGoy</u> at the <u>Hospice Maui</u> training program in October 2015.

Week Five: Exploring Regret

Ware, B. (2011, 2012) *The Top Five Regrets of the Dying: A Life Transformed by the Dearly Departing.* United States: Hay House.

Week Seven: Forgiveness

The concept of forgiveness involving reconciling how the past cannot change was something I heard from <u>Oprah Winfrey</u> on an episode of the Oprah Show many years ago, I can't place the exact episode, but it has always stayed with me.

Week Nine: Advance Directives

The referenced *Five Wishes* Advance Directive is available online at <u>AgingwithDignity.org</u>

Week Ten: Honoring Others

The thoughts regarding the importance of honoring our ancestors were inspired by the work of <u>Stephen Jenkinson</u>, but are not direct statements from him. He is the type of writer and speaker that seems to be impossible to summarize or paraphrase, yet has profoundly impacted the way I think. I highly recommend his book, "Die Wise: A Manifesto for Sanity and Soul" as well as listening to his lectures to hear his profound words yourself.

The power of considering all that our ancestors have sacrificed for us to be here was inspired by the introduction to a Sufi camp dance led by <u>Leilah and Bodhi Be</u>.

Week Twelve: Life Review

The ideas of Near Death Experiences and Life Review included in this chapter is a summary of what I've heard from others' personal experiences.

34748597R00047

Made in the USA
Middletown, DE
01 February 2019